FACING CHANGE

Falling Apart and Coming Together Again in the Teen Years

*We are all of us
all of the time
coming together and falling apart.
The point is, we are not rocks.
Who wants to be one anyway,
impermeable, unchanging,
our history already played out...*

Ted Rosenthal

**A Book About Loss and Change for Teens
By Donna O'Toole**

Compassion Press
Burnsville, North Carolina, USA

Published by
Compassion Press
7036 State Hwy 80 South
Burnsville, NC 28714
828-675-5909

ISBN 1-878321-11-0
Copyright © Donna O'Toole 1995
Revised and updated 2007

July 2007

10 9 8 7 6 5 4

Editing, layout and cover design by Therésa Müller
Photography by Wanda and Hannah Levin
Printed in the United States of America

Publisher's Cataloging in Publication
(Prepared by Quality Books, Inc.)

O'Toole, Donna R., 1939–
Facing Change : Falling apart and coming together
again in the teen years/Donna O'Toole.
p. cm.
Includes bibliographical references and index.
SUMMARY: A book to help young adults understand
the emotional, social, physical, cognitive and spiritual
impact of loss and change.
Includes bibliographical references and index.
ISBN-13: 978-1-878321-11-4
ISBN-10: 1-878321-11-0
1. Change (Psychology)—Juvenile literature.
2. Loss (Psychology)—Juvenile literature.
3. Grief—Juvenile literature.

1. Title.
BD637.C4086 1995   152.4
                              QB195-20479

CONTENTS
▼▼▼▼▼▼▼▼▼

CHAPTER
▼▼▼

PAGE
▼▼▼

I n the springtime, I remember the horse-drawn plow
cutting deep furrows through the prairie soil.
I can still experience and enjoy the smells of spring
including the freshly turned earth.
I can still see the robins and meadowlarks following the plow
to harvest the exposed earthworms.

C rises and grief are like that.
The blades of their pain cut deep channels
through our souls.
The plow also cuts the roots
of our comfortable beliefs and life-styles.
But, by the very turbulence,
it also prepares the soil to nurture new seeds.
These can take root and eventually flower in ways
that could not have been imagined before the soil
was so rudely prepared for new life.
The deeper the furrow cut by grief,
the more can flow through it. Fortunately
we can choose what runs in this channel to some degree.
At first it usually carries the torrent of our tears.
These can be followed by the acid flow of continuing bitterness
and resentment.
Or, gradually, we can let the living waters of compassion,
empathy, and love — ours and God's —
flow through this channel in our souls.
When this happens new flowering can be nurtured
in grief-parched lives — beginning with our own.

Howard Clinebell
Wellbeing — Growing Through Crisis

A NOTE FROM THE AUTHOR
▼▼▼▼▼▼▼▼▼▼

It would be easy to think that a book about loss and grief is a book about separation—about learning how to say goodbye. But saying goodbye is only part of finding your way through loss.

As we face change and find our way through grief, something more than goodbye happens: we remember the past ... we weave our lives back together ... we create connections.

Here's what seventeen-year-old Todd told me a year after his father had died: "I used to lay in bed listening for the garage door to open late at night. My dad worked a night shift and always came home after two in the morning. For months I stayed awake, listening for him. Not that I knew that's why I couldn't get to sleep. Then one night it just hit me: He's never coming back. `Dad. Dad,' I cried, `I want you to come home. Come home Dad. Come home.' No answer, no sound. So I yelled it again. My mother came running into my room. `What's wrong, Todd?' she asked. `It's Dad, Mom.

When your broken heart mends, you will no longer be the same. You will never be the same again. You will be stronger.

June Cerza Kolf

Teenagers Talk About Grief

He's not coming home—ever.' Then I cried and cried. I realized I was saying good-bye to him. The strangest thing is that, after I said good-bye to Dad, I started doubting that he was really gone. I knew he was dead, but he didn't seem gone. I started remembering all the things he liked and didn't like. I could even remember how his voice sounded. In a way Dad is still with me. I still talk to him. Lots of times I just wake up at about two-thirty in the morning, and say: `Hey Dad, what's up, old boy?'"

The point is that grief helps us know what is important to us, in the deepest of ways. Grief teaches us that the past can inform the future ... that love can transcend separation. This doesn't mean we get things back the way they were before the loss, or that we stay the same person we were before the loss. What it does mean is that by enduring the loss, by finding our own way through grief, new relationships and images can emerge. Grieving is how we create space for "new flowerings."

ABOUT CHANGE AND LOSS

Chapter 1

▼▼▼▼▼▼▼▼▼▼▼▼

Change is always with us. Sometimes you can keep change from happening, other times you are helpless to stop it. Some change is a natural part of growing up and some is sudden, unexpected and unwanted.

Whether a change is something you had hoped for, or something you didn't want to happen, it is likely that when it does happen, you'll also experience loss. Change and loss go hand in hand.

WHAT IS LOSS?

Loss means being without someone or something that was loved, familiar, important or desired. A loss can be a person, a place, an animal, an object, or even a dream or a hope—something that hadn't happened yet, but that you had 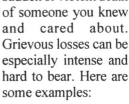 very much hoped for. Loss is the price we pay for loving, dreaming ... and for making attachments. Throughout this chapter you will see lists of some of the many losses young adults, like yourself, commonly experience. These lists are by no means complete, but they may help you recognize your own experiences of change and loss.

SOME LOSSES ARE EASY TO RECOGNIZE

Some losses hurt deeply and can leave you confused and disoriented— sometimes for a long period of time. Such losses may be easily recognized as grievous losses.

Grievous losses can be obvious, like an angry breakup with your boy or girlfriend, or like the death of a friend or close family member. Some grievous losses are traumatic, like the sudden or violent death of someone you knew and cared about. Grievous losses can be especially intense and hard to bear. Here are some examples:

- ▲ The accidental death of a classmate
- ▲ Death of a close friend
- ▲ Death of a brother, sister or parent
- ▲ Death of a close family member
- ▲ Death by suicide of a family member or friend
- ▲ Being sexually or physically abused
- ▲ Seeing someone murdered, raped or being abused
- ▲ Divorcing parents
- ▲ Living with alcoholic or abusive adults

7

SOME LOSSES ARE HARD TO RECOGNIZE

A loss is sometimes hard to recognize. Losses that are hard to recognize can also be hard to handle, because friends and family may not even realize the loss was important to you. They might think that you have quickly forgotten or "gotten over" whatever had happened.

Perhaps the change that happened was positive, something you had even hoped for. For instance: you may have wanted to move to a new neighborhood. You may be happy when you are finally able to make the move. At the same time you may feel sad and lost. The move may have meant that you had to leave behind familiar friends, family members, schools and neighborhoods. Many losses have parts that are positive and parts that are negative. These are examples of losses that may be hard to recognize:

▼ A best friend moves away
▼ A pet dies
▼ A brother or sister leaves home
▼ Your parents separate
▼ Being adopted
▼ Having your first sexual experience
▼ Losing a friendship
▼ Being robbed
▼ Losing a job
▼ Getting pregnant
▼ Having an abortion
▼ Having your driver's license taken away
▼ Wrecking your car
▼ A change in family finances
▼ Fire, flood, hurricane, tornado or other disaster
▼ New school, new teacher
▼ Parent remarries: new blended family
▼ Failing a grade or class in school
▼ Being injured or seriously ill
▼ Having someone seriously ill in your family
▼ Leaving school: graduating or dropping out
▼ Living with an alcoholic or other drug addicted family member(s)
▼ Losing an important dream
▼ Leaving home: beginning college.

EVERYDAY LOSSES MAY GO UNNOTICED

Some losses go by without being noticed at all. These are the losses that happen as a part of everyday life. Everyday losses may seem unimportant at the time they happen. But when everyday losses and hard-to-recognize losses accumulate, they can cause sadness, hopelessness and even depression. Here are some examples of everyday losses:

▼ Canceled dates or appointments
▼ Speeding tickets
▼ Put downs from friends, family, acquaintances
▼ Arguments
▼ Disruption of anticipated events
▼ Changes in family gatherings and celebrations
▼ Unavailability of parents, relatives or friends
▼ Lower grades than expected in school
▼ Broken promises
▼ Misunderstandings with friends
▼ A broken-down car
▼ Losing money or something else of importance

PEOPLE DON'T EXPERIENCE LOSS IN THE SAME WAY

Everyone is different. No two people will think or feel about anyone or anything in exactly the same way.

So no one can tell, for anyone else, what will be a minor loss or what will be a major and grievous loss that is hard to bear. The best we can do is to trust our own feelings about a loss and hope that others will trust us too.

MULTIPLE LOSSES ARE COMMON

Many losses are multiple losses. For instance, if you move to a new town you may also lose friends, teachers, neighbors, a familiar home and surroundings. If a brother or sister dies, your parents may be feeling so sad and confused that they are no longer there for you in the same way they used to be. Family traditions and habits may be changing, and a home that once felt comfortable may feel cold and empty.

WILL THE GOOD TIMES RETURN?

Facing losses can be challenging, but that doesn't mean you will never be happy again. Many people have gotten (and grown) through their losses. There are many things you can do to help yourself along the way.

WHAT IS LOSS?

Loss is physical.
*It can be felt as an ache in the heart,
a yawning emptiness,
and a lead weight that hampers
each movement.*

Loss is emotional.
*It is unyielding,
waves of tears
and violent undirected anger.*

Loss is mental.
*Your mind can be overtaken
by self defeating thought
and a lack of direction.*

Loss is spiritual.
*You question the meaning of life,
the existence of spirit,
and your own purpose.*

Yet it is through loss
*that we gain new meanings in life.
By embracing loss
we align with the rhythms and
cycles of our selves,
our living, and our world.*

Sydney Barbara Metrick
Crossing The Bridge

WHAT IS THIS THING CALLED GRIEF?

Chapter 2

▼▼▼▼▼▼▼▼▼▼▼

Grief is a natural and normal response to loss. It hurts to lose, but it helps to grieve. Grief can have many challenges and difficult experiences. Some people even call grief work.

HOW DO WE EXPERIENCE GRIEF?

Grief is a process that helps us adapt to change so that we can return to life with vitality and hope.

Grief is more than a feeling. We experience grief with our minds and our bodies. So don't be surprised if grief results in strong emotions as well as physical changes, and changes in thoughts, beliefs and habits. The lists below will give you some idea of the many different experiences grieving people often have.

COMMON FEELINGS DURING GRIEF

▼ Shock
▼ Numbness
▼ Disbelief
▼ Anxiety
▼ Fear
▼ Betrayal
▼ Emptiness
▼ Apathy
▼ Impatience
▼ Sadness
▼ Powerlessness
▼ Agitation
▼ Excitement
▼ Despair
▼ Uncertainty
▼ Shame
▼ Guilt
▼ Thankfulness
▼ Relief
▼ Loneliness
▼ Isolation
▼ Anger
▼ Strength
▼ Weakness
▼ Feeling uncared-for
▼ Feeling disconnected
▼ Uselessness
▼ Helplessness

COMMON MENTAL REACTIONS

▼ Difficulties in concentrating
▼ Continuously thinking about the loss
▼ Thinking that the loss didn't really happen
▼ Difficulty in making decisions
▼ Low self-esteem: feeling worthless
▼ Believing you were responsible for the loss
▼ Increased or decreased dreams
▼ Increased nightmares
▼ Thinking everyone watches you

▼ Thinking you are different from everyone else
▼ Self-destructive thoughts
▼ Creative expression through music, writing and art

COMMON PHYSICAL REACTIONS

▼ Tightness in the throat—having difficulty swallowing
▼ Shortness of breath
▼ Sleep changes: too little/too much
▼ Weight and appetite changes
▼ Tiredness
▼ Deep sighing
▼ Feeling weak
▼ Energized: feeling strong/ invincible
▼ Muscle tension
▼ Pounding heart
▼ Headaches and stomach aches
▼ Increased activity—can't sit still
▼ Decreased activity—no energy, loss of interest
▼ Increased sensitivity to sights/ sounds
▼ Temporary slowing of reactions
▼ Increased number of colds/ infections
▼ Taking on symptoms or behaviors of the person you are separated from or who has died

COMMON SPIRITUAL REACTIONS

▼ Feeling lost and empty
▼ Feeling forsaken, abandoned, judged or condemned by God
▼ Questioning a reason to go on living
▼ Feeling dislocated—as if you don't belong
▼ Questioning your religious beliefs
▼ Extreme pessimism or optimism
▼ Feeling the presence of God in your life
▼ Feeling the presence of the person who died in your life
▼ Needing to give or receive forgiveness
▼ Needing to give or receive punishment
▼ Feeling spiritually connected to what/who was lost

COMMON BEHAVIORS AND SOCIAL REACTIONS

▼ Searching for what was lost
▼ Withdrawing from friends and family
▼ Withdrawing from social activities
▼ Being constantly active
▼ Clinging
▼ Excessive touching or withdrawal from touch
▼ Seeking approval and assurance from others
▼ Aggressiveness

▼ Overachieving—trying to be super good
▼ Underachieving—trying to be super bad
▼ Changes in grades at school
▼ Being preoccupied and forgetful
▼ Being confused about time and space
▼ Bumping into people and things
▼ Crying
▼ Blaming others
▼ Being apathetic—dropping out

THE ROLLER-COASTER CYCLES OF GRIEF

Grief has been likened to a roller coaster ride, because it has many ups and downs. There are times when everything seems uphill, times when life chugs along in slow motion, times when life stands still, and times when your stomach seems to turn upside down because everything seems to be rushing by too quickly.

The different loops and cycles of the grieving process often overlap and blend into each other. It may help to know that others have traveled before you and have found their way back to safe ground. Here are some of the cycles they report:

▼ Shock, numbness and disbelief
▼ Avoidance and retreat
▼ Resistance, blaming and anger
▼ Constant thoughts of the loss

▼ Jealousy aimed at those who have what you do not
▼ Anger
▼ Self-blame
▼ Confusion and feeling disoriented
▼ Physical disturbances including exhaustion and changes in appetite and sleeping patterns
▼ Nervousness that includes pacing and fearfulness
▼ Sadness, longing and despair
▼ Reorganizing life, gaining new insights, learning new skills
▼ Increased awareness, understanding and forgiveness
▼ Feeling at peace with the past, wanting to be alone and quiet
▼ Increased sense of inner strength and competency
▼ Increased compassion and ability to listen to others
▼ Reconnection, resiliency, and hope for the future

GRIEF CAN BE HARD WORK

Since grief affects us mentally, emotionally, physically, socially and spiritually, it often requires considerable time and energy to work through. When you grieve you are working hard to make sense of the world. Your body is making many adjustments as you work with the emotions and the questions that help you adjust to the situation you are in.

A loss can sometimes be so great or so unexpected or overwhelming that it will threaten your ability to cope. You may never have experienced anything like this before. You might need some time just to get your bearings. You might need to figure out how to find or ask for support.

"It's hard work," said Aarvy Aardvark, as he worked to bury the beautiful blue bird.

"Yes ..." said Ralphy Rabbit, "But it is good work."

Donna O'Toole
Aarvy Aardvark Finds Hope

You may also find that working through your loss takes time away from the activities and relationships you used to enjoy. Sometimes the very things that used to make you feel physically and emotionally strong will remind you of your loss. Sometimes it just seems wrong to feel happy.

The emotions, thoughts and physical responses to a loss can be intense and demanding. Grief can make you feel as if you're from another planet: weird, confused and different from everyone else you know.

14

FINDING YOUR WAY THROUGH GRIEF

Chapter 3

▼▼▼▼▼▼▼▼▼▼▼▼

The intense emotions of grief can be likened to a storm. They can catch you unprepared and off guard. When a loss is great, you might fear the winds of the storm will pick you up and spit you out in a million pieces and that you'll never again come back together. But if coping skills are developed and used along the way, the storms can be navigated successfully.

GRIEF IS A CROOKED PATH

To find your way through grief is to walk a crooked path. Most people make it by going forward, backward, uphill and sometimes even in circles.

CREATIVE COPING

Coping creatively means finding safe ways to approach and then to encounter and tolerate the very thing that hurts. Coping means learning when and how to find shelter and support and when and how to walk headlong into the storm: when and how to face and when and how to avoid the loss. By using creative coping choices you can gain enough distance to muster up energy for the next part of the journey.

DEFENDING IS NOT COPING

Defending is a biological birthright. We instinctively respond to a sudden physical threat with defense: fight or flight. When we defend we attempt to beat someone or something into submission or into oblivion, or we are running away or hiding. A grievous loss feels a lot like a physical threat. But you can't run away from a loss, nor can you beat it up. And while people can and do sometimes bury their losses deep inside, they bury them alive, not dead.

Coping is the opposite of defending. Coping is learned through experience. Coping well requires skill and determination.

CREATIVE COPING MEANS HAVING CHOICE

People who cope well make use of a variety of coping choices. You can help yourself through grief by not getting stuck with only one or two coping options that already feel familiar or safe. Learning to use a variety of options can help you find your way through grief. Creative coping also means choosing consciously: being aware of what you are doing and why.

Using your coping options is a lot like learning how to juggle. You have to get the balls in the air and keep them going without losing them or getting too tired. And you have to learn how and when to put them safely away.

TWELVE COPING CHOICES YOU CAN USE CREATIVELY

Most people journey through loss by going forward and backward, by both experiencing the loss and by gaining refuge from it, by mixing periods of being in control, with periods of being vulnerable.

Seek information and get guidance from others

Reading books by, or having conversations with other people who have found their way through loss and grief,

may provide a kind of map that will help you work through your own process. By doing this you can learn that experiences you are having are natural and normal. But since not everyone gives trustworthy or applicable advice, you'll have to sort through and try out ideas to see which ones can work for you.

Share your concerns: find support and consolation

Seek or accept the concern and care of at least one other person who can understand your misery and soothe your sorrow. Sharing and accepting support also means validating that you may feel alone, but that you are cared for. Joining a support group of others who have losses similar to your own may help a lot.

Laugh it off: change the emotional tone

Some people use laughter falsely—as a way to avoid pain or to make jokes at other people's expense. But when used positively, laughter can be good medicine. Laughter is known to have positive chemical effects within the body. Laughter can actually reverse and release tension in your body and can give "time-out" from pain. Watch funny movies or read silly books.

Laugh with someone—not at someone. Laughing at someone is meant to ridicule that person and does not have the same positive benefits for releasing tension.

Distance yourself: put the loss temporarily out of your mind

Purposefully putting a loss out of mind is at times not only useful, but necessary. Worry or sorrow without rest can overcome the will to go on. The purpose of "consciously forgetting" is not to be indifferent to the loss, but to get enough rest so you can be involved in the daily activities of living. In other words, you take whatever you need before continuing on your journey.

Keep busy: involve yourself in meaningful activity

It is common to feel useless and unworthy after a loss. Being involved in something that gives personal satisfaction can be a way to feel needed, useful and valuable.

Confront the loss head on

This coping option is important to the grieving process. To continually avoid or distract the awareness of a grievous loss is to defend rather than cope. If you lack the emotional or physical safety to grieve, you may wisely choose defending against a loss until you can find enough support to use other coping options. But don't get caught in the helplessness trap. If you don't feel safe enough to grieve your loss, ask a counselor or a crisis hot-line for help. Build your support base. Confronting a loss isn't always about emotions. Having a remembrance ceremony or making something that expresses what the loss meant to you can be a way of mentally or physically confronting the loss.

Redefine the loss: look for the possible gain

With some losses this will be a hard option to choose. To redefine a loss is to rise above an unhappy situation by finding encouragement from within or without. It is to turn the loss around in your mind so it can be seen from other angles. This might include a heartfelt determination to survive the loss. You ask yourself, "What can I learn from this situation? What would it take to make lemonade out of this experience that seems so bitter and sour? Is there any deeper truth here at all?"

Accept that the loss has happened

This option lets you acknowledge that there are forces and situations beyond your control. It can also help you examine the things you do have choices about—what you can do differently in the future. Accepting that the loss has happened is important to the grief journey.

 ### Take action by reviewing alternatives

This option means thinking things through. It is not a spontaneous process, but does not necessarily mean prolonged reflection. Some questions to ask are: "What is left? What is worth doing now? How will I find out? Where will the different courses of action open to me lead?"

 ### Plan recesses: make a retreat

Grief is like swimming upstream. Sometimes you have to get out of the stream to find the strength to go on. A retreat isn't running away—it is a way to show compassion for yourself and for your desire to feel alive and well. You pull back in order to go forward. Some people do this by visiting some private hideaway that feels safe and secure.

 ### Conform: do what is expected or advised

This may be a difficult choice since it is natural to want to assert independence. Yet there are times when going along with someone else's ideas will give you the care, security or respect you need. And when a loss relates to a physical injury or an illness, it may be necessary to adjust to a prescribed treatment or physical limitation. Self-esteem requires a balance between getting your own needs and ideas responded to and responding to the needs and ideas of others. Look for signs of balance on your journey through grief.

 ### Express your grief: find ways to discharge feelings and tension

While getting feelings and tension out of your body may not always solve everything, it does allow you to clear out pressures that may be mounting inside. Expressing grief can include crying, yelling, throwing stones at telephone poles or hitting pillows. Or it may mean playing hard, dancing, running, writing poems or taking part in a sport. Releasing pent-up emotions can help you on your journey through grief. To let feelings out often requires courage and a safe and receptive environment.

CREATING A SUPPORT SYSTEM FOR YOURSELF

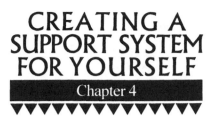

Chapter 4

▼▼▼▼▼▼▼▼▼▼▼▼▼

A GOOD SUPPORT SYSTEM INCLUDES VARIETY

It's easy to think of support as someone who will listen to your sadness. Yet, the friend who will sit with you in sadness may not be comfortable when you are angry or feeling down on yourself. And, the friend who can make you laugh may not be able to stick around when you cry. That's why it helps to think of support as a system, rather than as one or two friends or family members. Support systems can be made up of people, places and things.

Since grief affects the whole person, one way to think about support is to look at your physical, emotional, social and physical needs. The following surveys will help determine if you have an adequate support system, or if you need to build one. If your completed survey shows more blank space than completed space, you may want to take action. Ask a school counselor, parent or other trusted adult, or a friend to help you figure out how to increase your support quota.

MY SUPPORT SYSTEM

1. Name three people you feel comfortable to talk to:

_____Phone_____

_____Phone_____

_____Phone_____

2. Name a place you can go that feels comfortable and safe:

_____

3. Name three things you can do, or three people you can be with, to let out anger without hurting yourself or others:

_____

_____

_____

4. Name three things you can do, or three people you can be with, to let out sad feelings:

_____

_____

_____

5. Name three nonharmful things you can do to relieve anger and tension:

_____

_____

_____

6. Name three things you can do when life feels meaningless—when you feel hopeless and helpless:

_____

_____

_____

7. Name three activities you can do that will help you express your feelings. Examples: writing, drawing, chopping wood, hitting pillows, singing or playing music, dancing, playing a sport, working, pounding nails ...

_____

_____

_____

8. Name some things that help you get your mind off your loss:

_____

_____

_____

_____

9. List some things you did as a child that helped you through a difficult situation:

_____

_____

_____

10. List the names of songs you can play:

▲ To help me feel good _____

▲ To help me feel cared about and loved _____

▲ To help me with memories of my loss _____

_____

SUPPORT MEANS TAKING CARE OF THE WHOLE PERSON

Just as there are many different ways to cope, there are many different ways to look at and use support. Having a support system means finding a variety of resources to meet different emotional, mental, social, spiritual and physical needs. Resources often include people, places, music, books, movies, art and animals. Here's an activity to help you consider support for the whole person that you are.

SUPPORT FOR THE WHOLE ME

Physical	Mental	Feelings	Social	Spiritual

Instructions

1. Under each column heading, list at least five things that you could do to get support for yourself. These things could include people to talk to or just be with, places to go, things to do, or resources — such as books or movies — to give you new ideas.

2. Don't worry if you can't fill in every area right away: most people can't.

3. Make a copy of this page and ask some friends or trusted adults to fill in examples of things they do to help themselves through hard times. As you gather ideas from others, you'll be able to think of more things that you could choose to use as support for yourself.

22

75 THINGS YOU CAN DO TO HELP YOURSELF

▼▼▼▼▼▼▼▼▼▼▼▼▼

Although a loss can leave you feeling confused and helpless, there are many things that can be done to help you on your journey. If you've begun working on a support system, you already have a head start. This chapter has many more ideas. After reading through this list, you could choose five things to begin working on right away.

1. Keep a diary of your feelings. Read it over every couple of weeks or months to see how your feelings change.

2. Let yourself be angry: blow off steam. Get physical. Do it in a way, and/or with people that will assure your safety. Here are some ideas:

▼ Hit a big stack of pillows until you tire yourself out.
▼ Find a secluded spot: yell and scream to your heart's content.
▼ Play loud music and jump up and down until you wear yourself out.
▼ Write a note to the person you are mad at, then crunch up the paper and stomp on it.

▼ Write the name of the person you're angry at on the sole of your shoe. Rub your shoe sole back and forth in the dirt.
▼ Throw balls hard at a wall. Run to catch them. Do that until you're tired.
▼ Write the name, or description, of 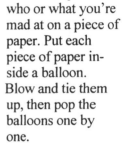 who or what you're mad at on a piece of paper. Put each piece of paper inside a balloon. Blow and tie them up, then pop the balloons one by one.
▼ Gather a bunch of old newspapers, magazines or phone books and rip and tear them up. Then stomp on the shreds, throw them in a garbage sack and away.
▼ Hit a punching bag.
▼ Get in a boxing match with referees present.
▼ Buy some old/cheap glasses or breakable plates at a rummage sale and throw them against a brick wall.

3. Don't be surprised or feel guilty if you can't or haven't cried. This is common. Let your feelings take their natural course and remember that there is no right way to grieve. Talk to someone about it if you are worried.

4. Cry if you want to. Why not? Crying can be a way to feel the loss—to know that it mattered. Tears are normal for people of all ages.

5. If you are feeling upset and afraid you'll become emotional in public (and you don't want to) ask a school counselor to help you develop a plan to have privacy without drawing attention to yourself.

6. If someone asks you how you feel, try to be honest. Don't say "I'm fine" if you're not. Say, "I'm feeling_____." But if you don't want to talk about your feelings it's OK to say, "Thanks for asking. I appreciate it. But I don't feel like talking about my feelings right now."

7. Inside balloons put slips of paper, each describing a feeling you want to get rid of. Blow up each balloon to a size that corresponds to the intensity of the feeling inside. Write the feeling on the outside of the balloon with a felt-tip marking pen. If the intensity of the feeling changes, let out air or add air and watch the feeling word shrink or grow. Tie the balloons up so you can play with them over time. This will help you see how feelings can and do change.

8. Write a list of the thoughts and feelings you are having right now. Then on three individual paper bags write
1. "Hold onto these for a while"
2. "Hold onto these forever"
3. "Crumple these up" or "Trash".
Cut your list apart and distribute each into a bag with an appropriate title. Every few days add to each bag or change the items from bag to bag as your feelings and thoughts change.

9. Share what you're learning from the balloon activity above with someone you trust and who will really listen to you.

10. Go for a long walk beside a river or stream. Notice the different signs of nature. Sit down and ask: "What does nature have to tell me about my situation?"

11. Share your thoughts and concerns with a good listener. (A good listener hears what you're thinking and feeling without interfering, judging or asking a lot of questions.)

12. Ask others for the names, addresses and phone numbers of people who have had a loss similar to yours and have gotten through it. Keep adding to the list. Keep the list available as a reminder that others have made it through great difficulty.

13. Call or write people on the list you made above. Ask them what they did that helped them cope and grow through their loss.

14. Ask the school or area librarian to help you find books about your loss. Read them.

15. Draw a set of three pictures with the titles:
  1. What my life was like before this loss
  2. What my life is like now
  3. What I want my life to be like someday
Show the drawings to someone who can agree to be a good listener. Explain the meaning of the drawings.

16. Draw a set of five pictures with the following titles:
  1. My loss
  2. Who I was before this loss
  3. Who I am right now
  4. Who I will be a year from now, and
  5. Who I will be five years from now
Show the drawings to someone who can agree to be a good listener. Explain the drawings and their meanings. Add whatever comes to your mind.

17. Ask for tutoring help if you have problems keeping up with your homework.

18. If you're doing well in school, but feel lonely, offer to do tutoring for some student that needs help.

19. Write to a pen pal and tell them everything. If you don't have a pen pal you can trust, write to an imaginary friend and tell everything.

20. Call a friend or a relative on the phone. If you don't know who to call, check the phone book to see if there's a crisis hotline service.

21. Help someone else.

22. Write a letter addressed to the person who has died, moved or whom you have lost. Tell them everything you are thinking. If you wish, watch the letter float away in a stream.

23. Write a letter to God. Say everything about the loss that is on your mind.

24. Visit the cemetery or the site of the loss, if it makes you feel better. If possible, leave some token of remembrance there.

25. Visit an old person whom you consider wise. Just go and listen to whatever they have to say.

26. Ask three different people who have gone through hard times and whom you admire, to tell you what helped them during hard times. Listen, and compare their answers to things that might work for you.

27. Visit a spiritual counselor, a minister, chaplain, rabbi or wise and kindly adult, and talk with them.

28. Find someone whom you like and who likes you. Do something with them.

29. Make a list of all the questions and things that concern you about the loss. Take your list to a trusted friend and ask them to help you figure out some answers.

30. Start a *Book of Memories*. Use a notebook, scrapbook or some paper stapled together. In it, put newspaper clippings, pictures, drawings, poems and notes related to your loss.

31. Make and decorate a *Memory Box*. Put special objects related to the loss inside. Keep the box in a special place.

32. Learn to process your loss in manageable doses. Light a candle for fifteen minutes each day, at a designated time to remember your loss. Then blow out the candle and do something different.

33. If the above does not appeal to you, then light a candle in memory of your loss only at very special times, for any period of time that feels right to you.

34. Plan a ceremony or memorial service that will pay tribute to the loss you experienced. Ask a family member or friend to help and to be with you.

35. Plant a tree in honor of your loss someplace where you can watch it grow. Give the tree a name that represents the way you feel about the loss.

36. Make or buy a piece of "memory" jewelry that can be a symbol of some part of the loss you wish to remember. Wear it daily for as long as you want. When you're feeling distressed, touch your fingers to the memory jewelry and ask for comforting thoughts.

37. Go to a funny movie and see it three times in a row.

38. Rent a bunch of funny videos and, if possible, watch them all night long with a friend.

39. Make a batch of chocolate chip cookies from scratch, and give some to someone who lives nearby. (You'll find the recipe on most chocolate chip packages.)

40. Remember that grief takes time. The questions and concerns you have right now may take some time to get answered.

41. Write five poems with the following titles:
1. My loss
2. Who I was before the loss
3. Who I am now
4. What helps a person face pain
5. Who I will be a year from now
6. What I will always remember

Make the poems into a special booklet with extra pages. A month from now, without re-reading the old poems, write new poems with the same headings. Compare the sets of poems.

42. Plan to be with a friend on special anniversary dates related to your loss, or do something special to comfort yourself or to remember.

43. Learn something new each day. Anything. Keep a daily record of what you learn. Read it over at the end of each week.

44. Use old magazines and newspapers to make a collage that represents all the different effects your loss has on you, or all the different things the loss means to you. Show the collage to someone who will listen while you explain its meaning.

45. If your loss is related to the death of a person or to some other separation from someone you cared about, do some good deed that would make that person really proud of you.

46. Remember it's not unusual to want to hide away after you've had a loss. But if you're feeling ashamed because you feel so strange, don't let that shame control your life.

47. If the loss was a person, talk to them as if they were with you now. Sit facing an empty chair and talk to the chair as if it were the person you're missing. Then move to the empty chair and talk back to the seat you've just left, as if you were that person talking to you. Move back and forth, talking, until you feel finished.

48. Write a short story or a poem about the experience you had with the empty chair, and share it with someone who is a good listener.

49. Let yourself off the hook. It's common to feel responsible for a loss. If you feel guilty, talk to a counselor about it. Ask them for suggestions that help people cope with guilt.

50. If you had a relationship break-up, it doesn't have to be a negative reflection on you. Ask, "What can I learn about myself and the other person from this?"

51. Certain songs may stir up intense feelings. Changing the radio station, or keeping the music on the shelf for a while, might help.

52. If you're concerned because you want to cry, but can't, try playing some music that reminds you of the loss and see if that helps.

53. Interview five adults or five friends. Ask them each to list five things they think are most important to do when one has experienced a loss. Compare the results and decide which ones you agree are the most important. Do these.

54. Remember that even though loss happens, love can be retained.

55. Grief takes time and grief takes its toll on your body and mind. Get adequate rest and eat healthy foods.

56. Do some active exercise for thirty minutes, at least three times a week, to help you feel better. If you don't know what exercise to do, ask your doctor, parent, counselor or gym teacher to help you decide. If sticking with an exercise routine is difficult, ask someone to help you by coming by to walk with you two or three miles, at least three days a week.

57. Join a support group. Your school counselor, clergy or parents can help you find the right one.

58. Ask your school counselor if your school has a peer counseling program. If so, try to join it. You might also want to read books from the library on peer counseling. They offer many good ideas.

59. Write a list of all the things about the loss that get you down and that you would like to be able to release. Place the list in an envelope or paper box and bury it somewhere so it can slowly dissolve in the ground.

60. Volunteer your time and services to someone or some organization.

61. Let yourself shift back and forth between facing and avoiding your loss. Few people can face all the pain of a loss all the time.

62. Talk to God. Decide on a meeting place and make a daily appointment to share whatever is on your mind. Talk out loud or write notes. Do this each day for at least a month.

63. Reread the list of coping choices listed in chapter three. Write down the ones you use the most. Then choose a new one to try out every day or two.

64. Ask a counselor or librarian to help you find videos or movies about someone who has grown through a loss like yours. Watch these. Write down the things that seem to help the characters on the screen.

65. Read the books *The Education of Little Tree*, by Forrest Carter, or *The Secret Garden*, by Frances Hodgson Burnett. Both are wonderful classics that deal with loss and hope.

66. Search for more information to help you understand why and how the loss happened. Your need for information is normal. Understanding helps you heal.

67. If your loss was sudden, violent or traumatic, recognize the following stress reactions and find someone to talk to if any of these are happening to you:
▲ startling at any noise or disturbance
▲ repeated nightmares
▲ excessive activity or a high degree of agitation that continues over time
▲ flashbacks: seeing the incident over and over
▲ an inability to remember the event that happened
▲ prolonged or intense difficulties in concentration and in making decisions

68. Schedule "times out" from grief—planned periods when you allow yourself to laugh, exercise or engage in life.

69. Remember this quote from George Bernard Shaw:
"Life does not cease to be funny when people die, any more than it ceases to be serious when people laugh."
Make a poster of this quotation and put it in a place where you'll see it every day.

70. Avoid the temptation to judge yourself too harshly. Don't tell yourself you're not handling this well. Chances are you're handling it as well as you can, given your circumstances.

71. Look for inspirational role-models. Study them for qualities you admire. Work at being like them.

72. Adopt an animal into your life—one you can hold, touch, hug and take care of.

73. Make a "brag list". This is a list of your positive qualities and actions that have gotten you this far in life and that can help you find your way through this loss.

74. Write a poem or draw a picture of a favorite memory about your loss. Frame what you have done specially, so that you can look at it and treasure it often.

75. You may be able to adapt and use many of the ideas and practical suggestions listed here. Whatever you do, one thing is certain: the journey you take through your loss will be like no other. It will be uniquely your own.

FINDING HELP USING HELP

Chapter 6

▼▼▼▼▼▼▼▼▼▼

Grief takes energy and effort. It can wear you out. That is why anyone going through loss needs support, practical help and encouragement.

Perhaps you are fortunate enough to have friends or family who can be there to share, help you gather information, and listen to you with interest and respect. But even if you have supportive friends and family, there are times when you may feel overwhelmed, fearful or unable to move ahead. Or you may be experiencing strange physical, emotional or behavioral reactions that may make it difficult for others to act sympathetically towards you. Finding help may be the most caring thing you can do for yourself during these times.

SIGNS THAT SUGGEST HELP MAY BE IN YOUR BEST INTEREST

▲ Continually being overactive, restless and agitated, without a sense of direction
▲ Noticeable changes in your personality that trouble you
▲ Inability to achieve goals
▲ Withdrawal from friends/family

for an extended period of time
▲ Drunk or reckless driving or other risk-taking behavior
▲ Extended changes in eating patterns that negatively affect nutrition and health
▲ Sexual activity to get attention, or to cover loneliness or fear
▲ Excessive use of alcohol or other drugs
▲ Physical symptoms such as headaches or stomach aches that linger
▲ Gradual or marked downward change in health
▲ Numbness to feelings over an extended period
▲ Feeling depressed and worthless and unable to motivate yourself to engage in a meaningful activity or social contact for prolonged periods
▲ Prolonged tension and agitation that keep you from sleeping
▲ Thoughts that life is not worth living, accompanied by thoughts about ending your life
▲ Ongoing problems in school such as skipped classes/dropped grades
▲ Explosive emotions that don't diminish. Fighting with friends or behaving hurtfully to others
▲ Extreme reactions of anger and guilt that persist over time

WHERE TO TURN FOR HELP

Perhaps you don't have a friend you can turn to. Or perhaps the friends you do have don't seem safe or available. You might have to do some looking, but luckily there are places to look. Below is a list of adults who are trained and have chosen to be of help. You may find it useful to think of these people as "professional" friends.

School Counselors

Many school counselors are trained to help people deal with loss and life transitions. School counselors sometimes hold regular support groups for teens experiencing loss. School counselors also know about other services available throughout the community that can be of help.

School or City Librarians

If you like learning about things on your own, books, videos and audio tapes about loss can help you understand the thoughts and feelings of grief and how others have successfully grown through loss. Ask a librarian to point you to the best materials to match your situation.

Local Health Department Nurses and Counselors

Look in your telephone book under Health Education and Referral Services. Health departments can provide information related to birth control, pregnancy, AIDS, nutrition, and many health and health education services. Most health departments have qualified counselors as well as medical people available.

Mental Health Counselors

Look in the phone book under Mental Health Services. Mental health facilities have a staff of professionals trained in helping people deal with any number of problems, including alcoholism and other drug abuse, suicide, depression, self esteem and various other losses. They often have telephone help-lines. You can make appointments yourself or through a school counselor, clergy, parent or other caring adult.

Clergy, Hospital Chaplains or other Spiritual Advisors

Churches, synagogues, mosques or other places of spiritual support have counselors who are committed to help. Many are trained mental health counselors as well as being trained to help with spiritual and religious questions.

Your Doctor

If you are lucky enough to have a family physician, this can be an excellent place to begin, especially since a physical checkup is recommended for anyone going through a major loss.

National Organizations and Websites

There are many national organizations that have chapters throughout the country. These organizations often have written pamphlets they can send free of charge. If you write or call, they can often provide the addresses and phone numbers for local chapters. A small number of such organizations is listed below. For additional organizations related to your specific loss, ask your school or city librarian.

▼ American Association of Suicidology

5221 Wisconsin Ave, NW
Washington, DC 20015
202-237-2280
www.suicidology.org

This association is a clearinghouse rather than a direct service agency. They will send pamphlets to survivors of a suicide and will provide referrals when possible.

▼ American Cancer Society (ACS)

1599 Clifton Road NE
Atlanta, Georgia 30329
404-320-3333
24-hour Information Center:
1-800-227-2345
www.cancer.org

An organization that provides information, services and support for cancer patients and their families. Ask about their *I Can Cope* program.

▼ Big Brothers—Big Sisters of America

230 North 13th Street
Philadelphia, Pennsylvania 19107
215-567-7000
www.bbbsa.org

This national organization has many local chapters. They can help teens in single-parent families find safe, caring adult companions.

▼ Center for Disease Control (CDC)

National Aids Clearinghouse
1600 Clifton Rd, Atlanta, GA 30333
800-311-3435
www.cdc.gov

A clearinghouse, providing referrals to support groups and services for those infected with HIV/AIDS, their caregivers and loved ones.

▼ Compassion Books, Inc.

7036 State Highway 80 South
Burnsville, North Carolina 28714
Phone: 828-675-5909
Fax: 828-675-9687
www.compassionbooks.com

A national resource center that gathers and sells over 400 books, CDs and videos to help people grow through losses of all kinds. Resource catalogs free upon request.

▼ Compassionate Friends

P.O. Box 3696
Oak Brook, Illinois 60522
877-969-0010
www.compassionatefriends.org

This organization for parents who have suffered the death of a child also has materials to help children and teens. They can tell you about local chapters, and supply booklets and pamphlets.

▼ Dougy Center

P.O. Box 86852
Portland, Oregon 97286
503-775-5683
www.dougy.org

A grief support center for young people who have lost a family member or friend, as well as losses related to suicide, accidents, and murder.

▼ Mothers Against Drunk Drivers (MADD)

511 E. John Carpenter Frwy,
Ste. 100
Irving, Texas 75062
800-438-MADD (6233)
www.madd.org

The MADD national office provides referrals to local chapters and supplies free brochures upon request. They can help teens become involved in programs to help prevent drinking and driving.

▼ National Hospice and Palliative Care Organization

1700 Diagonal Road, Suite 625
Alexandria, Virginia 22314
703-837-1500
www.nhpco.org

Hospice programs specialize in support to dying and bereaved people and families. They often offer grief support groups or educational meetings, and are an excellent resource for knowing about other community or area services in bereavement and life changes.

▼ TeensHealth

www.kidshealth.org/teens

This site offers lots of great information on your body, food and fitness, sexual health, drugs and alcohol, and diseases and infections. It also includes emotional issues such as school, jobs, and staying safe. Some information is available in Spanish. This site is specific to teens, so it's quite easy to find facts important to you.

▼ The Virtual Pet Cemetery

www.mycemetery.com

Create a memorial and message here for the pet you love.

Crisis Centers and Hotlines

Most city phone books have a list of public service agencies. Look in the front of the phone book under emergency numbers. A teen crisis hotline phone number is often listed. Also look in the yellow pages under Counseling Services, Mental Health Services, Social Services or Crisis Intervention for local telephone numbers to call.

If you need to talk to someone right now, but can't find the number of your local crisis center, call one of the national hotlines listed below.

▼ Covenant House Nineline
1-800-999-9999

Open 24 hours, 7 days a week. Covenant House, located in New York City, has a nationwide phone line to take calls from young people in trouble. The program primarily works with homeless youth who have run away, or who have been abandoned, but it also helps young people who are suicidal. The phone worker can give you immediate crisis intervention, or can use Nineline's listing of more than 24,000 agencies to find the crisis center nearest you.

▼ Girls and Boys Town
National Hotline: 1-800-448-3000
1-800-448-1833 (hearing impaired)

Open 24 hours, 7 days a week. Located in Nebraska, this hotline can be reached from all 50 states, Canada, Puerto Rico, and the Virgin Islands. Its trained counselors talk to more than 500,000 troubled and suicidal teens each year. The hotline's staff includes Spanish speaking operators. A TTY machine enables counselors to communicate with those who are hearing impaired. Using the hotline's database of more than 50,000 local agencies and services, Girls and Boys Town counselors can tell you where to find the crisis center or services nearest to you.

▼ National Association for Victim Assistance (NOVA)
510 King St, Suite 424
Alexandria, VA 22314
24-hour Hotline 800-TRY-NOVA
www.trynova.org

An organization that helps those who have lost a loved one through murder. They can provide advocacy for victim's rights and tell you if there is a chapter in a city near you.

▼ National Hopeline Network
www.hopeline.com

For the nearest Suicide Crisis Center: 800-784-2433

T here is a maple tree growing
in the woods near my home that I often visit.
It was many years before I realized that this tree,
and the story it tells, had taken on a special meaning for me.

A s a young sapling, the maple grew up
next to a barbed wire fence at the edge of a field.
Now, buried deep within the overgrown forest,
the tree has incorporated the remains of the barbed wire
within its sturdy trunk.
The wire does not simply graze the bark;
it is firmly embedded within the maple's core.
And yet the tree is majestic,
towering sixty feet above the undergrowth.

M y son loves this tree, and so do I.
We love that it lived on with such determination and strength
to tell its long-ago story of a sapling's encounter
with a sharp and potentially quite damaging obstacle
in its path.

Cynthia Monahon
Children in Trauma

BOUNCING BACK

Chapter 7

▼▼▼▼▼▼▼▼▼▼▼▼▼

◢ ⟍n the long run it's more healthy to deal with grief than to avoid it. Research shows that when grief is buried rather than experienced, it sooner or later surfaces as physical or emotional problems or limitations. Research also shows that people who are able to grieve their losses often gain understanding and maturity. They discover inner strengths they didn't know they had.

The ability to bounce back—even to grow through the painful losses of life—is called resilience. In this chapter you will find a list of clues that suggest your journey through grief is progressing ... that resiliency is in process. You'll also find some important ideas about the art and practice of resiliency.

25 WAYS TO KNOW YOUR JOURNEY THROUGH GRIEF IS PROGRESSING

◢ ⟍he signs of progress may be ever so slight at first. Yet even the smallest signs are important. They show that movement is taking place, that your efforts have not been in vain.

1. You realize some time has passed without your having thought about the loss.

2. You can concentrate on a book or on what others are saying again.

3. Your tears are less frequent.

4. Your anger is less frequent.

5. You make a new friend or reconnect with an old friend.

6. You can remember both pleasant and unpleasant memories related to the loss.

7. You can focus on the present rather than dwelling on the past.

8. You begin to think about, and to make some plans for the future.

9. Your school grades improve.

10. You can return to normal activities.

11. Your sleeping, eating and physical patterns are more like they were before the loss.

37

12. You don't feel so down on yourself.

13. You can feel warmth and affection again.

14. You notice your surroundings more.

15. You feel more capable of making decisions and solving problems.

16. Your humor returns.

17. You find yourself laughing again without feeling ashamed about feeling good.

18. The music you associated with the loss no longer has to be totally avoided, nor does it completely blow you away.

Working through grief is a little like working out for physical fitness. Those who lift weights cannot start with the maximum weight they hope to lift. They have to work up to these goals a little at a time.

Bob Deits
Life After Loss

19. You can give encouragement to others going through a similar loss.

20. You can listen to your friends again and feel concern for their needs.

21. You realize you have developed some new routines.

22. You no longer feel tired all the time.

23. You no longer feel agitated all the time.

24. You can feel the sunshine again.

25. You can remember without it hurting so much.

10 WAYS TO GROW THROUGH LOSS

Many psychologists have found that there are ways of being and behaving that help people grow—even through profound and abusive loss. From reading earlier sections of this book you may realize that you, too, have the ability to get through more than you ever thought possible.

The ten practices of resiliency listed below have been gathered from those who have studied how people bounce back from painful losses. These psychologists remind us that growth takes time and that most people learn these practices and ways of being a little at a time. But, they tell us, these traits aren't just for a chosen few. Their work over many years has convinced them that these traits are life skills. In big steps and in little steps, they can be learned.

1 Hopefulness

Resilient people have a determination and a desire that some good will eventually come from the painful experiences of the loss. When resilient people cannot feel hope from within, they look for others who can hold hope for them.

2 Awareness

To be aware is to be able to observe and experience thoughts and feelings rather than to interfere with, or censor them. Self-awareness is the ability to recognize physical and emotional needs and states.

3 Acceptance

Resilient people acknowledge and allow, rather than disown or deny, whatever feelings or thoughts emerge. They may at times doubt themselves, but they maintain a belief that they want and deserve to be loved and to be happy. Resilient people see their strengths, as well as their weaknesses, without being too critical. They reflect upon their actions and their feelings and then decide what to do.

4 Assertiveness

To be assertive is to be self-propelled. Resilient people express their wants and needs through words and actions. They say what they want and work to get it. To be assertive is to look for choices that will help you without harming others. Assertive people direct their lives, rather than accept whatever comes their way.

5 Friendliness

Resilient people are congenial. They connect with others. When hurting, they find others who care about them and who can help. Such people may be available for only brief periods of time, but the resilient person makes use of the kindness of others in their memory, visions and imagination.

 6 Active Imagination

An active imagination helps the resilient person dream and be receptive to new ideas and possibilities. This can help in solving problems and in finding the meaning of the loss and a hoped-for future. Those who are resilient construct and nurture positive visions, despite emotional disappointments.

 7 Kinship and Connections

Resilient people seek and find something or someone that gives meaning to their lives. They have some sense of kinship or commitment beyond themselves. Such connections can be found in being needed or in doing something to be of help to others.

 8 Remembrance and Commemoration

Resilient people remember and reassemble the past in order to understand how the loss fits into their lives over time. They commemorate a loss by recognizing, honoring or validating the past in some way. Planting a tree as a living memorial to remember a friend who died is one example.

 9 Forgiveness and Understanding

Resilient people seek to forgive or understand the circumstances surrounding the loss. They know that to forgive can release and transform the pain of the past. However, with some losses, (for example a murder or an unrecovered alcoholic parent) they may choose to suspend forgiveness because the person who caused the loss may not have changed their destructive behavior. In these cases, resilient people seek to understand what prompted the other person's actions, while learning to distance themselves from the emotional control the person who caused the loss has on their lives.

10

Life as a Story in Process

Resilient people have developed the belief that the events of their lives are a *part* of their story, but not *all* of the story. They are motivated to remember, understand, repair and integrate the past, rather than to forget it. They view the past, present and future as a continual unfolding—as a process. They understand that they do not "get over" a loss. Rather, they revisit the meaning the loss has to them at various times throughout their lives, so that they can better understand their present and future.

RESILIENCY DOESN'T HAPPEN ALL AT ONCE

To grieve is to practice the art of resilience. Just like any great work of art, growth through grief doesn't just happen. Resiliency and grief take time and effort. Both require skills and practice, and a great deal of perseverance. Yet the artists of grief are people just like you and me. They take the raw materials of life and create something of lasting value from them. The creations that are fashioned are not likely to happen all at once, nor are they likely to progress without discord. But gradually, ever so gradually, they are shaped and reshaped until they become whole.

"Real isn't how you are made,"
said the Skin Horse.
"It's a thing that happens to you ..."
"Does it happen all at once,
like being wound up," he asked,
"or bit by bit?"
"It doesn't happen all at once,"
said the Skin Horse.
"You become. It takes a long time.
That's why it doesn't often happen
to people who break easily,
or have sharp edges, or who have to
be carefully kept."

Margery Williams
The Velveteen Rabbit

The Mirror

I explain, "A lot of times people dream about the person. If you're open to it, I think it's a great way to stay in touch.

"I'm going to live my life for Fiona," Becky says. "You can't live anybody's life for them," I tell her.

"You can, though, live with their gift, and honor the gift. Fiona was such a great teacher for all of us. She was the mirror, reflecting us back to ourselves."

---

*A nd then after all our words, we dance.
We dance
And laugh
And cry
And remember.*

*Fiona had been a **wonderful** dancer.*

Jill Townsend
*from **Death is Hard to Live With**
by* Janet Bode

LAST WORD:
THE ART OF
GRIEVING
▼▼▼▼▼▼▼▼▼

Grief is not a problem to be solved: it is a process to be lived. Grief shows that we care about ourselves and about others. Grief doesn't forget life: it re-members it. Grief honors and validates the importance of the people we love, as it does the things, the ways of being human, and the dreams that matter to us. We find out who we are when we grieve. Grieving makes life count. It helps us gain vitality again.

Finding our way through grief is a lot like making a tapestry. A tapestry is a design or picture created by weaving many different threads together. The threads that make up a tapestry are of different textures and colors. As we grieve, memories of the past—of our losses—are gradually being gathered up, reclaimed and woven together into the present. Eventually a pattern emerges: a picture that shows that our past and present have been united.

To appreciate the art of tapestry is to look at it from both sides. The back of a tapestry can tell us about our brokenness. There we can see where all kinds of broken threads were left dangling and where they were securely tied together again. When we study the front of our tapestry, we see something quite different. We see the bigger picture. We see connections. We see the patterns and shapes of our lives having taken form. We might even see the beauty of our tapestry—regardless of the appeal that our particular design may (or may not) have to others.

To grieve our losses is to be an artist of life.

> *A new chapter can be woven out of the fabric of the old, the pain and struggle of the grief process itself, and the hopes for the future. The ability to grieve is also the ability to enjoy life!*
>
> Berta Simos
> *A Time To Grieve.*

READING
RESOURCES
▼▼▼▼▼▼▼▼

Some of the books below may be found in your school or local library. They may also be ordered through Compassion Books, 7036 State Hwy. 80 South, Burnsville, NC 28714. Phone: 800-970-4220.

▼ *Coping When Someone in Your Family Has Cancer*, Toni L. Rocha, New York, NY: Rosen Publishing Group, 2001

All aspects of dealing with cancer are addressed in this thorough book. It includes an extensive list of resources.

▼ *Coping With the Death of a Brother or Sister*, Ruth Ann Ruiz, New York, NY: Rosen Publishing Group, 2001

An excellent help with the emotional, medical, and practical questions that arise when a teen or preteen loses a sibling, this book includes a helpful glossary of terms and a resource list.

▼ *Coping with Teen Suicide*, James Murphy, New York, NY: Rosen Publishing Group, 1999

A book that gives good, clear advice to help recognize when a teen or his/her friend is at risk of suicide. Included is where and how to get help and how to deal with the loss of someone to suicide.

▼ *The Education of Little Tree*, Forrest Carter, Albuquerque, NM: U. of New Mexico Press, 1976

Through the wisdom of his grandparents and the renewing effects of nature, a young Cherokee orphan learns how to live life fully in this fictionalized account.

▼ *Everything You Need to Know About Grieving*, Karen Spies, New York, NY: Rosen Publishing Group, 1993

Large print and photos throughout add readability to this book about the experiences young adults may have after a loved one dies.

▼ *The Grieving Teen*, Helen Fitzgerald, New York, NY: Fireside, 2000

This wise, inviting handbook helps teens find answers to their specific needs. Complete with resource list of organizations and websites.

▼ *Help for the Hard Times*, Earl Hipp, Center City, MN: Hazelden, 1995

Cartoons, quotes and line drawings take youth on a hopeful journey through the many losses and challenges of teen life.

FACING CHANGE

▼ *Straight Talk About Death for Teenagers*, Earl Grollman. Boston, MA: Beacon Press, 1993

Easy-to-read information about what a teenager can expect following the death of someone close. Helpful suggestions are given throughout.

▼ *Teens Write Through It: Essays from Teens Who Have Triumphed Over Trouble*, Compiled by the editors of Fairview Press. Minneapolis, MN: Fairview Press, 1998

Fifty-eight teens who have faced and triumphed over profound challenges wrote these award-winning essays.

▼ *When a Friend Dies: A Book for Teens About Grieving and Healing*, Marilyn Gootman, Minneapolis, MN: Free Spirit Publishing, 1994

This book offers guidance on how you can cope with your sadness after the death of a classmate or friend.

▼ *When Nothing Matters Anymore: A Survival Guide for Depressed Teens*, Bev Cobain. Minneapolis, MN: Free Spirit Publishing, 2007

A survival guide for struggling teens, written by a mental health professional who has lived with depression and suicide.

▼ *When Someone You Know Has Been Killed*, Jay Schleifer, New York, NY: Rosen Publishing Group, 1998

This concise resource assists young people learn to heal and live fully after a violent death.

▼ *You and an Illness in Your Family*, Tabitha Wainwright, New York, NY: Rosen Publishing Group, 2001

Teens get answers on coping with the stress and changes that life-threatening or short term family illness creates. Multicultural photos add authenticity.

▼ *You and Violence in Your Family*, John Giacobello, New York, NY: Rosen Publishing Group, 2001

Real-life stories that show where and how help is found and received by young people and their families.

▼ *You Are Not Alone: Teens Talk About Life After the Loss of a Parent*, Lynne B. Hughes, New York, NY: Scholastic, Inc, 2005

What helps, what doesn't, and how to stay connected and begin healing after a parent's death. Thirty grieving teens and the author, founder of Comfort Zone Camp, tell their stories.

*What we call
the beginning
is often the end.
And to make an end
is to make a beginning.
The end is where we start from.*

T.S.Elliot
Four Quartets

BIBLIOGRAPHY
▼▼▼▼▼▼▼▼▼▼

▼ Bode, Janet. *Death Is Hard To Live With. Teenagers Talk About How They Cope With Loss.* New York, NY: Bantam Doubleday Dell, 1995.

▼ Clinebell, Howard. Wellbeing— *Growing Through Crisis.* New York, NY: Harper Collins Publishers, 1992.

▼ Deits, Bob. *Life After Loss.* Revised edition. Tucson, AZ: Fisher Books, 1992.

▼ Flach, Frederic. *Resilience: Discovering a New Strength at Times of Stress.* New York, NY: Fawcett Columbine, 1988.

▼ Kolf, Jane Cerza. *Teenagers Talk About Grief.* Grand Rapids, MI: Baker Book House, 1990.

▼ Metrick, Sydney Barbara. *Crossing The Bridge, Creating Ceremonies for Grieving and Healing from Life's Losses.* Berkeley, CA: Celestial Arts, 1994.

▼ Monahon, Cynthia. *Children and Trauma.* New York, NY: The Free Press, 1993.

▼ O'Toole, Donna. *Aarvy Aardvark Finds Hope.* Burnsville, NC: Compassion Press, 1989.

▼ O'Toole, Donna. *Growing Through Grief: A K-12 Curriculum to Help Young People Through All Kinds of Loss.* Burnsville, NC: Compassion Press, 1989.

▼ O'Toole, Donna. *Healing and Growing Through Grief:* Burnsville, NC: Compassion Press, 1993.

▼ Snyder. C.R. *The Psychology of Hope.* New York, NY: The Free Press, 1994.

▼ Schneider, John. *Finding My Way, Healing Transformation Through Loss and Grief.* Colfax, WI: Seasons Press, 1994.

▼ Weisman, Avery. *The Coping Capacity.* New York, NY: Human Sciences Press, 1984.

▼ Williams, Margery. *The Velveteen Rabbit.* Garden City, NY: Doubleday and Company, 1970.

▼ Wolin, Steven J. and Sybil. *The Resilient Self, How Survivors of Troubled Families Rise Above Adversity.* New York: Villard Books, 1993.

▼ Wong, Mary, editor. *The 1995 National Directory of Bereavement Support Groups and Services.* Forest Hills, NY: ADM Publishing, 1995.

Compassion Press

We publish only books that sing out
hope, without denying that life, as a journey,
has both challenges and choices.

Our other titles include:

Aarvy Aardvark Finds Hope
Growing Through Grief: A K-12 Curriculum
Healing and Growing Through Grief
Stories of Lead, Stories of Gold, CD
Panda Bear's Journey
Helping Children Grieve & Grow

Generous quantity discounts are available for Facing Change and our
other Compassion Press publications. Please contact us for more information.

We also specialize in gathering and distributing books, audios and videos
to help people grow through loss, change and grief.
For free catalogs, please call or write:

7036 State Hwy 80 South
Burnsville, NC 28714
828-675-5909
www.compassionbooks.com